ELLA HICKSON

Ella Hickson is an award-winning writer whose work has been performed throughout the UK and abroad. Her most recent play, *ANNA*, created with Ben and Max Ringham, opened at the National Theatre in 2019. *The Writer* and *Oil* opened at the Almeida Theatre in 2018 and 2017 respectively. In 2013–15 *Wendy & Peter Pan*, adapted from the book by J.M. Barrie, played to wide acclaim at the Royal Shakespeare Company. Other credits include *Riot Girls* (Radio 4), *Boys* (Nuffield Theatre Southampton/Headlong Theatre/HighTide Festival Theatre), *Decade* (Headlong Theatre/St Katharine Docks), *The Authorised Kate Bane* (Grid Iron/Traverse Theatre, Edinburgh), *Rightfully Mine* (Radio 4), *Precious Little Talent* (Trafalgar Studios/ Tantrums Productions), *Hot Mess* (Arcola Tent/Tantrums Productions) and *Eight* (Trafalgar Studios/Bedlam Theatre, Edinburgh). In 2011 Ella was the Pearson Writer-in-Residence at the Lyric Theatre Hammersmith and she was the recipient of the 2013 Catherine Johnson Award. She has been a MacDowell Fellow. She is developing new work for the National Theatre, the Old Vic and Manhattan Theatre Club. Her short film *Hold On Me* premiered at the 55th BFI London Film Festival. She is also developing various projects for TV and film.

Ella Hickson

SWIVE
[ELIZABETH]

NICK HERN BOOKS

London

www.nickhernbooks.co.uk

A Nick Hern Book

Swive [Elizabeth] first published as a paperback original in Great Britain in 2019 by Nick Hern Books Limited, The Glasshouse, 49a Goldhawk Road, London W12 8QP

Cover image: Sebastian Nevols

Designed and typeset by Nick Hern Books, London
Printed in Great Britain by Mimeo Ltd, Huntingdon, Cambridgeshire PE29 6XX

A CIP catalogue record for this book is available from the British Library

ISBN   978 1 84842 926 0

Swive [*Elizabeth*] was first performed in the Sam Wanamaker Playhouse at Shakespeare's Globe, London, on 6 December 2019, with the following cast:

PRINCESS ELIZABETH/   Nina Cassells
    WASHERWOMAN/
    KATHERINE GREY
QUEEN ELIZABETH/   Abigail Cruttenden
    CATHERINE PARR/
    MARY TUDOR
WILLIAM CECIL   Michael Gould
THOMAS SEYMOUR/   Colin Tierney
    ROBERT DUDLEY

WOODWIND   Sophie Creaner
CELLO   Maddie Cutter
PERCUSSION/MD   Zands Duggan

Writer/Creator   Ella Hickson
Director/Creator   Natalie Abrahami
Designer   Ben Stones
Composer   Angus MacRae
Assistant Director   Anthony Lau
Movement Director   Anna Morrissey
Associate Movement Director   Siân Williams
Globe Associate – Movement   Glynn MacDonald
Voice   Emma Woodvine
Costume Supervisor   Sian Harris
Candle Consultant   Prema Mehta
Consultant   Richard Pinner
Production Manager   Fay Powell Thomas
Stage Manager   Carol Pestridge
Deputy Stage Manager   Olivia Roberts
Assistant Stage Manager   Benedict Jones

Acknowledgements

My thanks to the cast, the creative and stage management teams, who offered their knowledge in the room and have been a huge help in the development of the script.

Thank you to Dr Will Tosh and the research team at The Globe.

My thanks to Michelle Terry and Jessica Lusk.

My longstanding thanks to The MacDowell Colony for providing the space and time to write.

My particular thanks to Natalie Abrahami and Anthony Lau.

Author's Note

This play aims to throw light on contemporary issues by looking through a historical prism.

Protestantism wouldn't have been referred to as Protestantism at the time, the life events of Mary Queen of Scots have been elided, John Knox's criticism of women in power appeared for the first time in Mary Tudor's reign. These choices, amongst others, exist in the service of the dramatic intention and themes of the play.

I would encourage future productions to engage with the work as a new play rather than as a history play.

E.H.

For Natalie

Characters

ELIZABETH Q [QUEEN]/CATHERINE PARR/
   MARY TUDOR
ELIZABETH P [PRINCESS]/KATHERINE GREY/
   WASHERWOMAN
SEYMOUR/DUDLEY
CECIL

This text went to press before the end of rehearsals and so may differ slightly from the play as performed.

Prologue

ELIZABETH Q. My mother seduced a man so successfully that he altered the constitutional history of this country. She staved off sleeping with my father for four years. When she finally took her knickers off, she lost everything. Including her head.

They executed her when I was three. They left me with a nursemaid, who fell asleep. It got darker and darker – and the candles were too high for me to reach.

Pause.

ELIZABETH P *appears.*

By the time I was fourteen.

ELIZABETH P (*panicked – whispered*). *Be merciful unto me, O God, my father, be merciful unto me; for my soul trusteth in thee; yeah, in the shadow of thy wings I will take my refuge, until these calamities be overpast.*

ELIZABETH Q. I hate the dark.

ELIZABETH P *drops to her knees.*

ELIZABETH P *prays – mutters, silently –*

The sense of history in this theatre, the cosy, candle-y Elizabethan feeling, is bullshit. The space is no more than five years old. What it creates, is a completely false sense of security.

The façade is removed.

ELIZABETH Q *goes to leave.*

ELIZABETH P *looks up, panicked.*

ELIZABETH P. Don't leave me.

ELIZABETH Q. –

ELIZABETH P. Please.

ELIZABETH Q. –

> ELIZABETH Q *leaves* – ELIZABETH P *reaches out for her – but* ELIZABETH Q *is gone*.

.

One

ELIZABETH P *prays.*

ELIZABETH P. *Be merciful unto me, O God, my father, be merciful unto me; for my soul trusteth in thee; yeah, in the shadow of thy wings I will take my refuge, until these calamities be overpast.*

Be merciful unto me, O God, my father, be merciful unto me; for my soul trusteth in thee; yeah, in the shadow of thy wings I will take my refuge, until these calamities be overpast.

Be merciful unto me, O God, my father, be merciful unto me; for my soul trusteth in thee; yeah, in the shadow of thy wings I will take my refuge, until these calamities be overpast.

Two

CATHERINE PARR *emerges – she looks at* ELIZABETH P.

CATHERINE. Elizabeth?

ELIZABETH P. My father is dead. He's left me. Hasn't he? Catherine?

CATHERINE. Yes.

Beat – ELIZABETH *tries to absorb it.*

Your brother is King. I've come to get you.

ELIZABETH P. Can I stay here?

CATHERINE. Not any more. You need to come and live with Thomas and me.

ELIZABETH P. Do you think he can see me?

CATHERINE. What?

ELIZABETH P. My father, now he is dead – do you think he can see me? Like God?

ELIZABETH *looks to the heavens, as if she's being watched.*

Do you think I'm pretty enough that he wouldn't have killed me?

CATHERINE. What?

ELIZABETH P. If I'd been one of his wives, would he have kept me or killed me – do you think? He kept you.

CATHERINE. Get your things.

Three

ELIZABETH P *and* CATHERINE *run around, having fun,*
CATHERINE *tries to catch her, trips her up.*

ELIZABETH P. I can hear Thomas, on the gravel.

CATHERINE. Can you?

ELIZABETH P. You smile when you know you're going to
see him.

CATHERINE. He's my husband, I love him.

ELIZABETH P. What was it like being married to a king?
When you were married to my father?

CATHERINE. Stop it. You need to get ready for your tutor.

ELIZABETH P. Tell me, please.

CATHERINE. You have Greek to learn.

Beat.

Good. Interesting. I liked it.

ELIZABETH P. Liked it?

CATHERINE. The parties and the dinners were interesting.

ELIZABETH P. I don't believe you. You hated the parties.

Beat.

CATHERINE. When he went away – and he left me as Regent,
I had to dispatch troops and they would kneel down in front
of me.

ELIZABETH P. If you would knight one, would you hold the
sword and *whop* – chop the head right off him.

CATHERINE. No.

ELIZABETH P. Did you get the clergy to do lectures in your
chamber?

CATHERINE. Don't get excited by the wrong things.

ELIZABETH P. What does that mean? (*Beat.*) Do you like this dress? Do you think it's pretty?

CECIL enters – he looks like he's carrying bad news.

CATHERINE. Mr Cecil?

CECIL. Dowager Queen Catherine.

CATHERINE. Sorry? Who let you in?

CECIL. One of your ladies.

ELIZABETH P. We thought we heard Thomas, it was you.

CECIL. Lady Elizabeth.

Pause.

CATHERINE. What do you mean 'Lady'?

ELIZABETH P. I'm Princess Elizabeth. You should call me Princess.

Beat.

CECIL. Can we speak privately?

ELIZABETH P. Has my brother cut me out of the succession?

CATHERINE. Elizabeth. To your tutor.

ELIZABETH P. Tell me.

No one speaks.

Do you like my hair, Mr Cecil?

CECIL. It's charming.

CECIL touches her, lightly on the chin.

ELIZABETH P. You're not allowed to touch me. I'm a princess.

CECIL. It was only lightly.

CATHERINE. Now.

ELIZABETH P. My stepfather, Lord Admiral Seymour likes it.

Four

Later.

SEYMOUR *sits,* CATHERINE *is on his lap.*

ELIZABETH *watches.*

CATHERINE *attends to him, smooths his hair – kisses his face.*

CATHERINE. Your hands are cold.

SEYMOUR. They're alright.

CATHERINE. And your nose.

SEYMOUR. I've been –

CATHERINE. At the pub?

SEYMOUR. Me?

CATHERINE. I don't believe it for a second.

They kiss.

SEYMOUR. The fourth time she married for love and they were very happy.

CATHERINE *takes his hand and puts it on her belly.*

CATHERINE. The nurse today, took one look at me – and said it was a boy.

SEYMOUR. Did she?

CATHERINE. She did.

SEYMOUR *rubs it, he's pleased.*

SEYMOUR. I don't think I can do another day kneeling in front of a ten-year-old king. He told me to congratulate you on your handwriting.

CATHERINE. What?

SEYMOUR. The last letter you sent him, he said to tell you – he was particularly pleased with your handwriting.

CATHERINE. He's ten. He can hardly fucking read.

SEYMOUR. Careful. They'll do you for treason.

Up – I need to go and get changed.

SEYMOUR *exits*.

CATHERINE *sees* ELIZABETH P.

CATHERINE. Were you spying?

ELIZABETH P. I can't sleep. Will I still have my tutor if I'm only a lady? Or will they take him from me?

CATHERINE. Come here – you're shaking.

CATHERINE *holds* ELIZABETH P.

ELIZABETH P. I had a bad dream. (*Beat.*) I was lonely.

CATHERINE. I love you. Thomas and I – we love you. Your brother, the King, loves you.

ELIZABETH P. Does he?

CATHERINE. Of course he does. He's threatened by you, that's all.

ELIZABETH P. I tried to light the candles, but I couldn't reach them. It's so dark.

CATHERINE *holds* ELIZABETH P *to her – really hard*.

CATHERINE. You're okay. Do you hear me?

ELIZABETH P. You're crushing my hair, careful.

CATHERINE *goes to hug her again*. ELIZABETH P *steps back*.

What's a whore?

CATHERINE. What?

ELIZABETH P. The maid said my mother was a goggle-eyed whore and that's why she won't repair my dress with holes in it.

CATHERINE. What was her name? The maid?

ELIZABETH P. I don't want to get her in trouble.

CATHERINE. If anyone ever says anything like that to you again.

ELIZABETH P. –

CATHERINE. You look at them, straight in the face – and you remember who you are and then you turn away. With dignity, do you hear me?

ELIZABETH P *nods*.

Five

ELIZABETH P. *Be merciful unto me, O God, my father, be merciful unto me; protect me – look over me, guide me, for my soul trusteth in thee; yeah, in the shadow of thy wings I will take my refuge, until these calamities be overpast.*

SEYMOUR *enters.*

SEYMOUR. You can't sleep?

ELIZABETH P. Not really.

SEYMOUR. You ever see the dawn in?

ELIZABETH P. Sometimes.

SEYMOUR. I bet that's / lonely.

ELIZABETH P. / Pink, these days.

SEYMOUR. That bit just after three where no one is awake and everything gets too –

ELIZABETH P. Even though you know it'll be alright in the morning.

SEYMOUR. But when it's night and no one is there.

ELIZABETH P. Yeah. It all gets – huge.

SEYMOUR *nods.*

SEYMOUR. You could ask one of the lady's maids to sleep next to you – in your room.

ELIZABETH P. They don't like me.

SEYMOUR. I'm sure they do.

ELIZABETH P. Not like they like you. Someone sleeping, when you're awake is lonelier than there being no one at all.

SEYMOUR. Is it?

ELIZABETH P. Is Catherine sleeping?

SEYMOUR. She is.

ELIZABETH P *smiles at him, it's coquettish – he likes it, warmth – a moment.*

ELIZABETH P. It's strange talking to you when you're in just your nightshirt.

SEYMOUR *looks down at it, like he's only just noticed it.*

SEYMOUR. Sorry. Try not to look at it?

ELIZABETH P. Okay.

SEYMOUR. What were you reading?

ELIZABETH P. Calvin.

SEYMOUR. Tell me.

ELIZABETH P. 'Since the creation of the world, we see just as the days and months increase and multiply, so similarly, little by little, by succession of time the mind of man is more ingenious and inventive, more adorned and polished, than it formerly was.'

SEYMOUR. So we get smarter as we get older.

ELIZABETH P. The mind of man is more inventive by the succession of time.

SEYMOUR. So we get smarter as we get older.

ELIZABETH P. Succession. Newer is better. I think.

SEYMOUR. Do you?

ELIZABETH P. I do.

SEYMOUR. I like talking to you. It's not like talking to anyone else.

ELIZABETH P. Maybe it's because I'm new.

SEYMOUR. Youth's great downfall is its hubris.

ELIZABETH P. I thought the young were valued for their ambition. And.

SEYMOUR. And?

ELIZABETH P. Spirit.

Beat – they smile – they seem oddly equal.

I like your nightshirt.

SEYMOUR *laughs.*

Why are you laughing?

Beat.

SEYMOUR *strokes the side of* ELIZABETH P*'s face.*

SEYMOUR. You still have those soft little hairs. Can I touch you?

ELIZABETH P. Uh. I don't know.

SEYMOUR *steps towards her – she steps back.*

ELIZABETH P *puts her flat palm on the bottom of* SEYMOUR*'s belly.*

I do this to Lady Catherine.

SEYMOUR. She's pregnant.

ELIZABETH P. Is that exciting? Having a child.

SEYMOUR. Yes. It is. I think you should take your hand away.

ELIZABETH P. It is a boy – I can feel it.

ELIZABETH P *removes her hand.*

It feels different to how a woman feels.

SEYMOUR. You've never touched a man before?

ELIZABETH P. No.

SEYMOUR. You wanted to?

ELIZABETH P. It feels different, to a woman, it is harder, in the same place. Warmer. Maybe.

SEYMOUR. We should go hunting. If it's your favourite.

ELIZABETH P. God. God is my favourite. God is always my favourite.

SEYMOUR. You like to hunt?

ELIZABETH P. Yes.

SEYMOUR. Why?

ELIZABETH P. If I listen, I can hear the deer, in the trees –

SEYMOUR. And?

ELIZABETH P. To sense a thing and be sure of it – without seeing, then to have it proved – and shoot it.

>ELIZABETH P *steps towards him, she's nervous – but she holds his gaze.*

>ELIZABETH P *takes his wine from him.*

SEYMOUR. You want some wine?

>ELIZABETH P *looks at the cup, she looks at* SEYMOUR.

ELIZABETH P. Take this, all of you, and eat it – For this is my body which will be given up for you.
Take this, all of you, and drink from it:
For this is the chalice of my blood,
The blood of the new and eternal covenant.
Which will be poured out for you and for many
For the forgiveness of sins.

>SEYMOUR *is oddly moved. He kneels – she feeds it to him; he drinks – 'Amen'. He's made little – he likes it. He stumbles, he's unpicked.*

SEYMOUR. I'm drunker than I realised. I should go to bed.

ELIZABETH P. Sorry.

SEYMOUR. Don't be sorry. Sometimes you seem fourteen. Others you absolutely don't.

ELIZABETH P. I like talking to you.

Six

CATHERINE. You wrote to Cecil asking him for advice. I didn't give you permission to do that.

ELIZABETH P. –

CATHERINE. You asked him how you should be addressed?

ELIZABETH P. Yes.

CATHERINE. Why?

ELIZABETH P. I wanted to know if there was a way that I could still seem close to the throne. He suggested I refer to myself as the King's sister. So that people would know who I am by association.

CATHERINE. There isn't anyone in this country who doesn't know who you are.

ELIZABETH P. –

CATHERINE. You wrote to Dudley?

ELIZABETH P. How do you know about my letters?

CATHERINE. You asked him for money for new dresses?

ELIZABETH P. He's a friend.

CATHERINE. We give you dresses.

ELIZABETH P. If I don't spend it on dresses, I can give it to you to help pay for my tutor.

CATHERINE. So it hasn't already been spent?

ELIZABETH P. I kept it.

CATHERINE. What for?

ELIZABETH P. Just for safety.

> ELIZABETH P, *silent in her secrecy.* CATHERINE *looks at her, not sure to trust her.*

CATHERINE. Thomas said you put your hand on his stomach.

ELIZABETH P. To see if he had a baby.

CATHERINE. He can't have a baby – he's a man.

ELIZABETH P. I was just –

CATHERINE. Yes?

ELIZABETH P. I didn't mean anything by it. It was a game.

Beat.

CATHERINE. I think what you think you portray is innocence – but I don't buy it.

ELIZABETH P. I'm not trying to portray anything.

CATHERINE. The way you curl your hair.

ELIZABETH P. Is the way my hair curls.

CATHERINE. You pull bits of it down at the side.

ELIZABETH P. My eyesight isn't good. I can't always see what I'm doing.

CATHERINE. You smile at him. I've seen it. You're bright – and involving.

ELIZABETH P. Is that a bad thing? You've always taught me to be /

CATHERINE. / Don't use your intellect against me. I gave it to you.

Beat.

You're incredibly bright, Elizabeth – you know exactly what you're doing.

ELIZABETH P. –

CATHERINE. You tilt your head to the side when he's speaking, you widen your eyes, to let him know you're really listening, you blink like an innocent victim. You are too smart for all of it.

Beat.

ELIZABETH P. And what if I'm not doing any of that – and it's just what you're seeing?

CATHERINE. I have loved you since you were a child, and love you still. This situation is not my preference.

ELIZABETH P. What harm does it do – even if it were true? Which it isn't. It's okay to be nice to people, to listen. No?

CATHERINE. It's insecurity that's making you do it and you have no need of it.

ELIZABETH P. You stare at me more than he does. You look at my legs when I'm getting changed. You always tell me how lovely my skin is. You watch me when I wear something new – the shape of my arms when they're bare. You stare at me. You can't help it. People stare at fourteen-year-olds. You're forty. It's different.

CATHERINE. I'm not sure I can be a good guardian to you, any more.

ELIZABETH P. He comes to me. In the night, when he can't sleep. I can't ask him not to. I don't know how.

Pause.

CATHERINE. You'd be better in other lodgings.

ELIZABETH P. You promised you would look after me.

CATHERINE. If he comes to you – it is because he feels welcome. Encouraging lust in men is an aggression. It costs you nothing. It's invulnerable. It's a performance.

ELIZABETH P *looks at* CATHERINE *straight in the eyes, she remembers who she is – and turns away – without saying anything.*

Seven

Darkness, the Tower. ELIZABETH P, *alone, she's terrified, she can hardly breathe from panic.*

ELIZABETH P. Please don't kill me, please don't kill me, please don't kill me – please, please – please don't kill me, please don't kill me, please. (*Screaming.*) Let me out! I don't want to be in here! Let me out!

Be merciful unto me, O God, be merciful unto me; for my soul trusteth in thee; yeah, in the shadow of thy wings I will take my refuge, until these calamities be overpast.

The door is opened.

No! No – you can't take me. Not at night, you can't do it secretly – if you're going to kill me you have to do it in daylight where people can see that you're killing a princess. No! You can't take me!

CECIL *enters*.

CECIL. Elizabeth.

ELIZABETH P. You can't take me.

CECIL. I'm here to help you.

ELIZABETH P. Don't touch me.

CECIL. I think you've been wrongly accused.

ELIZABETH P. Thomas came to me, he came to me in the night-time. I swear it.

CECIL *nods*.

My brother wants me dead. He wants to be rid of me. He's using this as an excuse. Ask Lady Catherine – I spoke with her about Thomas. She knows. Make her tell the truth.

CECIL. The Privy Council think you started an affair with Thomas Seymour so that you could get pregnant and make a claim for Edward's throne. They think it's treason.

ELIZABETH P (*uncontrolled, reaches for the door*). Let me out! Let me out! Let me out!

CECIL *lets her calm down – waits for her to settle.*

This was my mother's cell. The jailor told me.

CECIL. The day she was executed – I looked after you. You were only little, they left you in the nursery and I sat with you. All day.

ELIZABETH P. I never touched Thomas.

CECIL. They will need convincing.

ELIZABETH P. Ask Lady Catherine! Ask her! Ask Lady /

CECIL. / Calm down. Please. I can't ask her. She died in childbirth.

Pause. ELIZABETH P *stands – entirely alone, she can't stand it.*

ELIZABETH P. Did she ask for me?

CECIL. I don't know.

ELIZABETH P. Did she name the child?

CECIL. Yes. Mary.

ELIZABETH P. There's no one then.

CECIL. There are sketches on your Greek papers of male limbs.

ELIZABETH P. Limbs?

CECIL. Legs. A man's legs.

ELIZABETH P. Heracles. Greek.

CECIL. Thomas Seymour is renowned for his /

ELIZABETH P. / Is he?

CECIL. The Council has the papers and is using them as evidence.

ELIZABETH P. I loved Catherine. She was the only person who ever made me feel safe.

CECIL. You don't want the throne?

Beat.

ELIZABETH P. I want to go home but I don't know where it is.

CECIL. Elizabeth?

ELIZABETH P. Please. Please, Cecil – don't let them kill me, please?

ELIZABETH P puts her hand on CECIL's chest – she almost doesn't realise she's doing it, until she's done it. She looks at it. CECIL looks at it. She removes it, quickly – like it's been a mistake.

CECIL. Marry him.

ELIZABETH P. Who?

CECIL. Seymour is now widowed. If you make the plea, clearly, that your intentions were only ever romantic and that nothing ambitious or political ever passed between you. That it was love and only love – and as such, personal – and unstoppable. They will let you marry him and retire to the country – it will take you both out of circulation and stop you from being a threat. You'll keep your head.

Pause. ELIZABETH P thinks.

ELIZABETH P. Will you arrange for me to present myself to the Council?

CECIL. That I can do.

ELIZABETH P. Thank you.

CECIL turns to leave.

Cecil?

CECIL. Yes?

ELIZABETH P. Will you get a new dress to me?

CECIL. It will be in your favour to look as if you are suffering.

ELIZABETH P. They won't notice.

CECIL. Then why /

ELIZABETH P. / It will work.

Beat.

CECIL. Your brother is ill.

ELIZABETH P. How ill?

CECIL. Your sister /

ELIZABETH P. / Is going to be Queen.

CECIL. I'm just warning you.

CECIL *exits*.

ELIZABETH P *prays*.

ELIZABETH P. Let us not be weary – but strong and of good courage for in due season we shall reap, if we faint not. (*Beat*.) I pray for you to teach me – I can bear anything if I can see the lesson in it. I will learn it.

Eight

ELIZABETH P *stands in front of the Privy Council.*

ELIZABETH P. Gentlemen of the Privy Council. Thank you for
seeing me. I wanted to speak, to explain. Lord Seymour did
come to me. He encouraged me to marry him with a view to
taking the throne from my brother. I told him, repeatedly,
that such a thing was treason and I wouldn't do it. I would
have no part in it. I love and am loyal to, my brother, the
King. Seymour, in his arrogance and gross ambition,
persisted. I can only, now, confess his guilt for him.

CECIL. Thomas Seymour, First Baron of Sudeley, executed for
treason by beheading.

SEYMOUR *is executed.*

Nine

MARY *enters*.

MARY. You tried to attack me.

ELIZABETH P. –

MARY. I'm your sister and you tried to attack me.

ELIZABETH P. –

MARY. You have no loyalty. You tried to unseat our dear
stepmother, by fucking her husband – and then you tried to
unseat me, as soon as I was Queen.

ELIZABETH P. I didn't.

MARY. I have letters, in your handwriting, written by you – to
the French Ambassador giving your support to their attempt
to kill me.

ELIZABETH P *stares* MARY *in the eyes – she shakes her
head solemnly*.

Why should I believe my tricksy little sister? With her pretty
little face – and her lovely little waist.

ELIZABETH P. You are with child. It is a time for celebration.
You are newly married. All I feel for you – is joy.

MARY. I see. And the letter?

ELIZABETH P. Is a forgery. It's commonplace. I have been
misrepresented. I wanted to see you to congratulate you on
your marriage to King Philip.

MARY *shows* ELIZABETH P *her ring*.

It's lovely.

MARY. It's a boy. The baby. Emperor and the Pope himself
have said so.

ELIZABETH P. Can they tell? All the way from Rome?

MARY. In their wisdom they can see all things.

ELIZABETH P *kisses her sister's hand.*

ELIZABETH P. Don't send me back to the Tower, I'm innocent.

MARY *swallows – can't quite bear it. Wipes her own face of sweat.*

MARY. The heat. In here.

ELIZABETH P. You should rest.

MARY. Take mass with me.

Pause.

ELIZABETH P. My faith is my being – were I to betray it, I wouldn't have much need for the life that I'm begging for – so. It would be God's will.

MARY. Take mass with me.

Pause – ELIZABETH P *won't do it.*

You think it's integrity but you're just stubborn. Your 'serenity' – is nothing but the arrogance of Protestant self-assertion. It's not conviction, or faith, it's the insecurity of someone who can't hear any view that is different to their own, in case it unsettles them.

ELIZABETH P. There's strength in conviction.

MARY. It's bloody-minded.

ELIZABETH P. You burn heretics. I can smell them on the evening wind from my cell.

MARY. When you were three, our father lifted you onto his shoulders, and paraded you through Court. I remember, how delighted you were by the attention. You danced without anyone having to ask you to.

ELIZABETH P. That's normal for a three-year-old.

MARY. You were desperate to have your portrait painted.

ELIZABETH P. I don't remember.

MARY. The charm has no effect on me, it reminds me too much of your mother. You have her eyes – they're black.

ELIZABETH P. No one has black eyes – it's a myth.

MARY. They're black. I can see them.

ELIZABETH P. They're dark brown. If that.

MARY. The only truth there is in you is your ambition.

ELIZABETH P. I have a clarity about my purpose on earth, as a princess should – it is inherent in me. There is no reason for me to be ashamed of that divinity.

MARY. I am your Queen!

ELIZABETH P. And as such your power is God-given – and, as we speak, you are trying to push a bill through Parliament that gives away your power to your husband.

MARY. You get much news in your little cell.

ELIZABETH P. Listen to me /

MARY. / You're here, as a traitor, to beg for your life.

ELIZABETH P. You've stalled on having him coronated properly, you've had your throne built so it's a few inches taller than his, you have yourself served from gold and him from silver, you know that you are a Sovereign Queen and he is only a foreign prince – you *know* it – and still you give it away. You hand it over to him – you ask his opinion on everything. At the theatre, I am told, you look to him before you laugh or gasp – to see what he is doing. To seek permission for your reaction. When he barely speaks English.

MARY. He is my husband. I am obedient to him. He is the King.

ELIZABETH P. You exceed him in age and rank.

MARY. Our strength is our unity.

ELIZABETH P. Where is Philip? He should be here – if you're about to have his child, shouldn't he?

MARY. You don't sleep, do you? You've always been so full of doubt. You doubt yourself, dreadfully.

ELIZABETH P. Where is he?

MARY. Your mother didn't understand the sanctity of marriage so you don't either and it's a tragedy because it's a security that you, of all people, could benefit from. I want to see you at peace.

ELIZABETH P. He's in Spain. Isn't he? Philip?

MARY. If there was someone to share your bed – who could comfort you. It must be so lonely, to set yourself apart from everybody, in the way you do.

ELIZABETH P. I think the reason that I can't sleep is because I've spent most of this year imprisoned in the Tower for a crime I haven't committed. The child in you, was meant to arrive two months ago. You're ten weeks overdue. The church bells were rung, in error, on the due date but had to be silenced because no baby came. Half the ambassadors in Europe are waiting downstairs for a child that isn't going to arrive. What is inside you is an illness, that is going to kill you and you cling to it being a baby because you won't permit the truth.

Long pause.

Your husband is nowhere to be seen.

MARY. Stop it.

ELIZABETH P. I'm the only one who will come up here and tell you the truth. To live so deep in – does the darkness comfort you? (*Beat.*) You will die and your husband will come to me, days afterwards and ask for my hand in marriage. You have signed away the right for English queens to rule, in perpetuity, to a man who is playing tennis and fucking lady's maids in Spain, whilst you are screaming his name from your deathbed.

MARY. Don't you dare marry him. I will kill you before you marry him.

MARY dies.

Ten

ELIZABETH P. For in due season – we shall reap if we faint not.

CECIL *enters*.

CECIL. I advised that you should retire to the country – take yourself out of circulation and stop yourself from being a threat.

ELIZABETH P. Since the creation of the world, we see just as the days and months increase and multiply, so similarly, little by little, by succession of time the mind of man is more ingenious and inventive, more adorned and polished, than it formerly was.

CECIL. So we get smarter as we get older.

ELIZABETH P. The mind of man is more inventive by the succession of time – succession – newer is better.

CECIL. The Queen is dead. Queen Mary is dead. You are much grown and serious.

CECIL *touches her lightly – on the chin*.

ELIZABETH P. You can't touch me – I'm a queen.

ELIZABETH Q *enters*.

CECIL. Long live the Queen. Long live Queen Elizabeth.

ELIZABETH Q. Where are the jewels? Don't leave me.

ELIZABETH P. –

ELIZABETH Q. Please.

ELIZABETH P *leaves*.

CECIL. The jewels are in the room next door, hair comes at five.

ELIZABETH Q. Ladies-in-waiting /

CECIL. / Given the instruction about the /

ELIZABETH Q. / When?

CECIL. They'll be here just after six. Not suggesting, of course, that you have any need of it. The carriage will pick you up half an hour later and deliver you through the front courtyard into the great chamber where pretty much every ambassador in Europe will be waiting for you.

ELIZABETH Q *thinks a minute.*

ELIZABETH Q. They've put the sun on the carriage? They got the message to do that?

CECIL. Maternalism. Fecundity. Radiance.

ELIZABETH Q. Benevolence.

CECIL. Indeed.

ELIZABETH Q. I want to see the jewels. I want to see what suits me. I want you to be my Principal Secretary.

CECIL *bows, humbly.*

You will not be corrupted by any manner of gift?

CECIL. I will not.

ELIZABETH Q. You will give me counsel that you think is best – and if you show me anything necessary to be declared as secrecy, you shall show it to myself only?

CECIL. I will.

ELIZABETH Q. And you swear absolute loyalty?

CECIL *nods.*

CECIL. Now, please, they are starting /

ELIZABETH Q. / Cecil?

CECIL. Yes? What? Excuse me – I mean /

ELIZABETH Q. / I was never in the Tower. Not for the rebellion against Mary, they never imprisoned me.

CECIL. But you /

ELIZABETH Q. Nor for the Seymour – thing.

CECIL. But /

ELIZABETH Q. / Do you understand?

CECIL. I think I do.

ELIZABETH Q. I was never removed from the succession by my father or my brother.

CECIL. I – see.

ELIZABETH Q. My sister – Mary.

CECIL. Is dead, you are Queen.

ELIZABETH Q. She will be known for cruelty; she was unintelligent and oversubmissive to a Spanish King and to the Papacy. Her imagined pregnancies disguised the truth of the tumour that killed her. I will be known as the first Sovereign Queen.

CECIL. Your Majesty, you cannot just rewrite history.

ELIZABETH Q. Yes, I can. I'll wear a really big dress, with shiny things on it – and we'll just repeat it, frequently.

CECIL *turns to leave*.

Don't you dare turn away from me before I've finished.

CECIL *turns back. A little diminished*.

CECIL. You are the first Sovereign Queen.

ELIZABETH Q. And the powers for female monarchs that my sister signed away will return to me.

CECIL. Tomorrow morning we can discuss this, right now we need to /

ELIZABETH Q. / Cecil, I have asked you to be my Principal Secretary and not my Regent. I am not fifteen. You will listen to me when I want to be listened to.

CECIL. We will try and revoke the constitutional limitations that your sister put in place. (*Beat*.) Your Majesty? King Philip of Spain has offered you his congratulations and his hand in marriage.

ELIZABETH Q. I can't hear you.

CECIL. Sorry?

ELIZABETH Q. Sorry?

CECIL. Is that a – yes?

ELIZABETH Q. What?

CECIL. What?

ELIZABETH Q. Who?

CECIL. Your Majesty – please, answer me.

ELIZABETH Q. Is that the time.

CECIL. I'm not sure I /

ELIZABETH Q. / I'm terribly sorry.

CECIL. The King's proposal.

ELIZABETH Q. I can't quite hear you.

CECIL. I've been quite clear.

ELIZABETH Q. I'll be back in a minute.

CECIL. Your Majesty?

ELIZABETH Q exits, she disappears.

CECIL is left standing – briefly.

For fuck's sake.

CECIL follows ELIZABETH Q.

ELIZABETH P enters, picks up some discarded clothes and becomes WASHERWOMAN.

WASHERWOMAN. We walked down to the river to see her Coronation, the new Queen. People were stood ten deep. I only saw a couple of inches of the carriage over everyone's heads. Me and the girls in the laundry, do her sheets – I hold them up, sometimes, thinking – she's slept on this.

I went to Thames Street to see if I could catch a look – her face. The dress, the jewellery – the way they'd done her up. It's madness, all these rubies – the money – seriously. She was waving. Sort of at everyone – sort of at no one, she doesn't actually know anyone.

I thought she might look nervous, or something. She didn't. She looked – incredibly pleased with herself. This smile on her. The way she waved – like arrogant – like, it had always been due to her. Nothing soft or gentle... I know I'm not meant to say this about a queen but it made me not like her very much.

WASHERWOMAN *picks up some sheets – and exits.*

I'll keep cleaning her sheets though, obviously.

Eleven

ELIZABETH Q *bursts back onto the stage, as if she's left the party in a rush.*

ELIZABETH Q *is pulling at the front of her dress like it's too tight.*

ELIZABETH Q (*hardly heard*). It's too tight. I can't breathe.

DUDLEY *enters.*

DUDLEY. You alright?

ELIZABETH Q. Robert.

DUDLEY. You need to get back in there. To start the dancing. They're waiting.

ELIZABETH Q. Tell them to start without me.

DUDLEY. Elizabeth.

ELIZABETH Q. Dudley?

DUDLEY. You're the Queen.

Beat.

ELIZABETH Q *looks at him.*

ELIZABETH Q. Do you think I look like one?

DUDLEY. Have you seen what you're wearing?

ELIZABETH Q *notices it – looks at* DUDLEY, *she's unconvinced.*

You're fine. Come on.

DUDLEY *puts his arm out to take her in.*

ELIZABETH Q. You're not allowed to touch me. Not without permission.

DUDLEY, *hands off –* ELIZABETH Q *moves past him.*

You should kneel.

DUDLEY *half does.*

Twelve

KATHERINE GREY *in audience with* ELIZABETH Q *in her Privy Chamber*.

ELIZABETH Q. Katherine Grey, you genius, you found some. Have you had a good evening?

KATHERINE. Yes. It's been wonderful.

ELIZABETH Q. They were all saying you're beguiling, but look at you.

KATHERINE (*slightly unconvincing*). There is no sun brighter than you, Your Majesty. Your radiance is unparalleled. The way you looked, this evening.

ELIZABETH Q. The neckline on this – is – did you wear this dress when you were serving under Mary?

KATHERINE. I was told you wanted us to wear things that were slightly more.

ELIZABETH Q. Do you like it?

KATHERINE. I. I mean I chose it so /

ELIZABETH Q. / I think it's very appealing. The way it – (*Mimes.*) whilst you were dancing tonight. Everyone was looking.

KATHERINE. I'm glad you like it.

ELIZABETH Q. I saw you, with the Spanish ambassador.

KATHERINE. What? Sorry. Pardon.

ELIZABETH Q. The smiling and the thing you do with your head, on one side – to show you're listening, and this little grin – slightly off-kilter – to affect innocence, it's very charming. It makes him think you're impressed but don't really understand, so he just keeps speaking and speaking.

KATHERINE *stares at* ELIZABETH Q, *completely nonplussed*.

KATHERINE. I think that's just how my face works.

Beat.

ELIZABETH Q. There are women who will tell you that doing such things makes you look stupid.

KATHERINE. Really?

ELIZABETH Q. They'll judge you, harshly; you flirt to cover the fact that you're not very interesting. Is what they'll say.

KATHERINE. That's sort of true. Maybe. (*Laughs, kindly.*) Ha. I'm terrible at books. My sister was better.

ELIZABETH Q. Lady Jane.

KATHERINE. Yes.

ELIZABETH Q. I think it's good that you have an effect – on men.

KATHERINE. Is it?

ELIZABETH Q *and* KATHERINE *laugh, conspiratorially.*

ELIZABETH Q. Do you miss your sister?

KATHERINE *nods.*

KATHERINE. I have this nightmare where I see her being executed all over again, the way she was scared and stumbled and reached for the block with her hands but couldn't find it because they'd put the blindfold on too early.

ELIZABETH Q. How old was she?

KATHERINE. Seventeen.

ELIZABETH Q. They killed her because she reached for the throne.

KATHERINE. She was Queen. For a couple of days. At least.

Strange silence between them – KATHERINE *is unsure of her footing.*

ELIZABETH Q (*small beat*). I think it's wonderful that you're sparkly and smiley and bring joy. If you make an ambassador or two grin, brighten up his day – well, what can be the harm? There's enough grimness to endure, isn't there?

KATHERINE *nods, still solemn – still a little unsure.*

(*Quietly.*) There are people who call it witchery.

KATHERINE. Call what – witch – what do you mean?

ELIZABETH Q. The effect you have on men.

KATHERINE. I've never done anything to do with witchcraft, ever, Your Majesty.

ELIZABETH Q. I know. All I'm saying – it's a power. Isn't it? It's like a game of chess.

KATHERINE. I don't know chess, I've tried to play but I'm bad at it.

ELIZABETH Q. You're young and beautiful and I think we should use that. Courtiers will give you information, very easily, and when you get it, I want you to come and tell me. Okay?

KATHERINE. I – what sort of things? Do you want me to tell you?

ELIZABETH Q. Some of the people at the moment, are panicking, about there being a queen and no king and we just need to keep an eye on it. You and me. The panic. Stop it from – bubbling. So, just listen to what they're saying. Then – come and tell me. Just between us, okay?

KATHERINE *nods, fearful.*

I'm going to move you from the bedchamber to the presence chamber so that you're more – amongst it all.

KATHERINE. That's a demotion, from where Mary placed me.

ELIZABETH Q. Are you objecting? Was my sister's policy your preference?

KATHERINE (*swallows, shakes her head slightly*). No, Your Majesty.

ELIZABETH Q. Why don't you go back through? I think they're still dancing. Have some fun.

KATHERINE. What if they catch me. Listening?

ELIZABETH Q. You're working for the Queen. No one can make you safer. Let us be educated and use our assets as best we can? Doesn't that sound like security? You've got such soft skin, like a peach.

KATHERINE *nods – nervously, and goes to leave.*

Katherine?

KATHERINE. Yes?

ELIZABETH Q. Just talking. Take it no further. To fuck without my permission, is treason.

KATHERINE *exits.* ELIZABETH Q *stares.*

Thirteen

CECIL. Because there are things I don't need to bother you with.

ELIZABETH Q. But there is a persistent need to discuss the suit of King Philip?

CECIL. He's waiting for an answer and he's one of the most powerful men in Europe.

ELIZABETH Q. The plan for today is to discuss the drafting of the Act of Supremacy.

CECIL. Philip wants his answer.

ELIZABETH Q. If we get the drafting of the Act of Supremacy right, and it goes through – then I will be the Supreme Head of the Church, like my father.

CECIL. Indeed.

ELIZABETH Q. We will, in religious terms, be separated from Rome.

CECIL. Yes.

ELIZABETH Q. So why, when we've just worked very hard to detach ourselves from subservience to one Catholic power, would I enslave myself to another by marrying King Philip?

CECIL. I'm not sure Supreme Head will go through. Parliament, maybe, Lords – we will struggle.

ELIZABETH Q (*small beat*). Well then, we need to apply ourselves more rigorously to the bill's drafting, don't we?

CECIL. I would suggest Supreme Governor.

ELIZABETH Q. My father was Supreme Head.

CECIL. Governor has a more – protective and nurturing ring about it. It is more – generous-sounding.

ELIZABETH Q. And Head is?

CECIL. There's something – officious and overbearing /

ELIZABETH Q. / My father was Supreme Head and it made him sound powerful.

CECIL. We want to tread carefully.

ELIZABETH Q. He didn't.

CECIL. The situation is different – it needs different terminology. There are people that will struggle, a little, with the idea of a – we need to tread carefully and help them, get used to – Governor starts with a 'G' – it is a round letter, it's softer – it hints to fecundity.

ELIZABETH Q. Does it?

CECIL. You could be Supreme Head if you married Philip. I get the sense, that the people would accept it, if you were married.

ELIZABETH Q. Why?

CECIL. Supreme Head and queen with no king – is too /

ELIZABETH Q. / Too?

CECIL. As I say, we just need to tread carefully.

ELIZABETH Q. Didn't you suggest Ascham, as my tutor, when I was young?

CECIL. What's that got to do with /

ELIZABETH Q. / He taught you – Ascham did? Didn't he?

CECIL. We were at university at the same /

ELIZABETH Q. / Your wife is one of the smartest women in England. One of the Cooke sisters, famously well-educated, all but an in-house seminary. No?

CECIL. Yes.

ELIZABETH Q. You spend your days between the two smartest women in England.

CECIL *raises his eyebrows.*

Am I wrong? Is that inaccurate? Are we – Mildred and I – well-educated?

CECIL. Yes.

ELIZABETH Q. Smarter than you? (*Long pause*.) Is your wife smarter than you? Am I?

CECIL. Sometimes I get these memories of you – terrified, at fifteen – and this new Queen is a total surprise to me.

ELIZABETH Q. Don't do that. (*Pause*.) We're discussing a Parliamentary issue, I'm not sure it's appropriate or useful for you to be thinking about when I was scared and fifteen. I don't look at you – as the years draw on – and imagine an old man sitting, uselessly, by the fire – do I?

Beat.

CECIL. I thought we shared a friendship.

ELIZABETH Q. I'm only asking a question. Am I smarter than my father was?

CECIL *nods, very slowly – uncomfortably*.

Then why was he Supreme Head and I have to settle for Supreme Governor? Which is, whatever rounded letters mean, a demotion. And yet, I'm allowed Supreme Head if I marry a Catholic king? Can you explain that to me, Cecil?

Fourteen

ELIZABETH Q *appears, covered in blood.*

DUDLEY *enters – sees her – panics.*

DUDLEY. What have you done?

ELIZABETH Q. Nothing.

DUDLEY. You got away from me.

ELIZABETH Q. Where are the rest of the hunting party?

DUDLEY. I told them to wait. You're covered in blood.

ELIZABETH Q. I heard a deer in the trees, I sensed it and shot it. I found it and it was squealing and so I cut its throat and took its heart out.

Beat.

DUDLEY. You need to clean your hands or there will be a fuss.

DUDLEY *takes off his scarf – or similar.*

ELIZABETH Q *puts out her hand – asks for it.*

ELIZABETH Q. I'll do it.

DUDLEY *doesn't give it.*

ELIZABETH Q *asks.*

DUDLEY. No. I'll do it.

ELIZABETH Q *resists – eventually lets him – he cleans her hands.*

One might say thank you.

Beat.

ELIZABETH Q. How is your wife, how is Amy?

DUDLEY. Is that why I'm not King?

Beat – she doesn't respond.

I don't know how my wife is. My employer won't release me to go and see her and I'm not allowed to have her at Court.

ELIZABETH Q. You can go home if you want.

DUDLEY. I don't want.

ELIZABETH Q. A man should want to see his wife.

DUDLEY. This man wants to see you.

She holds his eye for a moment – but can't quite take it – she looks away.

Beat.

ELIZABETH Q. We should head back. The hunting party /

DUDLEY. / What is it about me that unsettles you?

ELIZABETH Q. Nothing.

DUDLEY. We've known each other since we were children and you still can't look me in the eye.

ELIZABETH Q. I'm due in Council.

DUDLEY. Unless you've had wine and then you can't take your eyes off me.

ELIZABETH Q. Cecil thinks I should send you away – to marry Mary Queen of Scots.

DUDLEY. I'm married. Remember. And I'd rather not.

ELIZABETH Q. So, you don't want to be King?

DUDLEY. Scotland's very far away. And cold. I like it here.

ELIZABETH Q. They say she's prettier than me.

DUDLEY. That's not only inaccurate, it's impossible. Your eyes, they're black.

ELIZABETH Q. It's a myth. You should know better than that.

DUDLEY *steps towards her. She steps back.*

DUDLEY. You let Cecil rule you.

Beat.

ELIZABETH Q. There are negotiations between Cecil and I that you aren't privy to. He often declares what we've already privately agreed.

DUDLEY. I found him in the pub one night after he'd had a few, he told me – in some detail – about how much he wants to fuck you and what he thought it might be like.

ELIZABETH Q. You can't speak to a queen like that.

Beat.

DUDLEY. I'm just telling you what he said.

ELIZABETH Q. And what did you say back?

DUDLEY *shakes his head – as if to say 'nothing'.*

I am Queen.

DUDLEY. You like watching bear-baiting; you smile when they get ripped apart.

ELIZABETH Q. What would you do – if you were King and I was Master of the Horse?

DUDLEY. Execute you.

ELIZABETH Q *laughs.*

I'm joking – it's a joke.

ELIZABETH Q. At the Tower, under Mary, when they brought you through the Traitors' Gate – you must have known they were planning to kill you and you were grinning.

DUDLEY. Was I?

ELIZABETH Q. There is something unkind in you and yet all you ever speak is niceness.

DUDLEY. You're imagining a threat that isn't there because it keeps people clear of you.

ELIZABETH Q. Am I?

DUDLEY. Just before you killed that stag, you thought you were alone, you seemed, so fierce – and complete. Then

I made a noise and you turned and saw me and suddenly, all that ferocity turned to fear and not because of the kicking, screaming, thing in front of you – but because I'd interrupted you. I'd made you feel less free.

He steps towards her – she steps back.

You can accept amorous admiration, but you prohibit desire. Why?

ELIZABETH Q *breathes, looks at him.*

ELIZABETH Q *goes close – to kiss him – breaks away.*

ELIZABETH Q *exits.*

Fifteen

ELIZABETH Q. What did you just put in your pocket?

CECIL. Who?

ELIZABETH Q. You.

CECIL. Me?

DUDLEY *enters*.

ELIZABETH Q. If you show me anything necessary to be declared as secrecy, you shall show it to myself only. Not keep it and hide it.

DUDLEY. What's going on?

CECIL. You stink of booze.

ELIZABETH Q. Answer the question. There are twenty men – and I have just watched you pass round a letter, of some description – so that every man has read it – or has been made aware of it – and Hatton just passed it back to you.

CECIL. Why don't we discuss this privately?

ELIZABETH Q. No, you're fine – these things can be discussed publicly – we're looking towards transparency, to make everyone feel a bit more comfortable. Aren't we?

CECIL *passes* ELIZABETH Q *the piece of paper*. ELIZABETH Q *reads it*.

DUDLEY *stares at* CECIL.

CECIL. What are you looking at?

DUDLEY. You haven't shown it to me.

CECIL. You were late.

ELIZABETH Q *passes the pamphlet to* DUDLEY.

DUDLEY. This is circulating on Cheapside. Why haven't you shown her this before now?

CECIL. So you knew about it and didn't show her either?

ELIZABETH Q. What possible reason did you have, Cecil, for showing this to every one of my councillors before showing me?

Beat.

DUDLEY. She asked you a question.

CECIL. I don't think she needs you to speak for her.

ELIZABETH Q. 'She'?

DUDLEY *and* CECIL *look to her.*

(*Reads the pamphlet.*) 'To promote a woman to bear rule, superiority, dominion or empire above any realm, nation, or city, is repugnant to nature. A thing most contrary to God's will. It is a subversion of good order, equity and justice. It is monstrous. A female ruler can only retain power by a combination of seduction and witchcraft and so doing debases her male subjects.' Do you feel debased? Do you?

CECIL. 'Men are more suited to rule; it doesn't mean women can't rule. It is quite clear that God ordained Elizabeth to rule when he provided no male heir. It is plain that for some secret purpose God has decided Elizabeth should govern.'

Beat.

I was waiting until everyone had signed off on the counterargument, before I showed it to you. Being presented with a problem, without the offer of a solution, is unpeaceful. I was trying to –

DUDLEY *scoffs, audibly.*

Dudley? Can you tell us why you were late?

DUDLEY. I had a problem with my horse.

CECIL. You live on the Strand. We're in Whitehall. Are you drunk?

DUDLEY. No. More than usual.

Life is long, Cecil. You know the only time I've ever seen him cry is when he was moved by one of his own very moving stories.

CECIL. Robert Dudley's wife – Amy Robsart has been found dead this morning at the bottom of the stairs with a broken neck and two large gashes in her head.

Pause.

DUDLEY. You think it's okay to tell me that in here?

CECIL. I presumed you already knew.

DUDLEY. How did she die? Did she fall?

CECIL. Did she?

CECIL *steps back – and avoids it.*

DUDLEY. Are you accusing me?

CECIL. She was severely ill. Her bones were weak. She may have fallen. One of her maids heard her praying, desperately, the night before for salvation from her pain.

DUDLEY. She took her own life?

ELIZABETH Q. That is a mortal sin and it will not be discussed in /

CECIL. / She was found at the bottom of only eight stairs with the coverchief on her head still exactly in place – it seems unlikely, to me that – and then there are the two gashes in her head, which would take some explaining.

Beat.

DUDLEY. You're talking about my wife. I'd be grateful if you weren't so casual.

ELIZABETH Q. This won't be discussed in Council.

CECIL. It needs to be. He is a councillor and there will need to be an investigation. A trial. Right now, Your Majesty, for your own safety – we need to ask him to leave.

DUDLEY. When was she found?

CECIL. This morning.

DUDLEY. When was she last seen alive?

CECIL. Yesterday evening.

DUDLEY (*turns to* ELIZABETH Q). So, you know it wasn't me.

Pause – ELIZABETH Q *flushes*.

CECIL. There are cartoons circulating through the courts of Europe showing that the Queen of England has rejected King Philip so that she can marry her Master of the Horse. They are not becoming. This new – information – about Robert Dudley's wife will damage the Crown.

ELIZABETH Q. Surely Europe knows that Robert Dudley is a homely cup and were the Queen to marry him she would start a civil war, what with every blacksmith and stable boy in the country thinking they too could be King. He should leave.

DUDLEY *injured – moves away.* ELIZABETH Q *can't look at him.*

DUDLEY. He's – he's – isolating you – I promise you. It wasn't me.

CECIL. Her Majesty has spoken.

DUDLEY. I'm leaving.

CECIL *stands firm*.

ELIZABETH Q. Council is dismissed.

Everyone leaves – except for CECIL. ELIZABETH Q *sits – stares*.

You too. You can leave.

CECIL. Europe is laughing at you – about Dudley.

ELIZABETH Q. Humiliated? Just before they try to kill me. That's how it goes isn't it?

CECIL. Why does Dudley think you're his alibi for the middle of the night?

ELIZABETH Q. Dudley's wife was much more likely to have been murdered by someone wanting to blacken his name than she was by Dudley himself.

CECIL. I hope that doesn't have direction in it.

Pause – ELIZABETH Q *doesn't respond.*

The cartoons use a word that likens you to your mother.

Long pause.

ELIZABETH Q. You can leave.

Sixteen

KATHERINE GREY and CECIL *whisper – we can't hear what they're saying*. CECIL *appears to be in control of things*. KATHERINE *is charming*. KATHERINE *puts her hand on* CECIL's *chest* – CECIL, *beguiled, laughs*.

KATHERINE. Your grace.

CECIL. Katherine, is everything well?

KATHERINE. I –

CECIL. Tell me.

KATHERINE. I wondered if – there's, I have a letter /

CECIL. / For Hertford?

KATHERINE. How do you /

CECIL. / Give it to me – I'll make sure he gets it.

Seventeen

THE PEOPLE OF ENGLAND. 'A petition presented by the English people to the most noble Queen Elizabeth of England and the High Court and Parliament. If you, O Queen, do die void of issue and wanting of a known successor and ordered succession, as the case now standeth, what good can continue? What evil shall not come? It is uncertain whether you shall marry. It is uncertain whether you shall have issue in your marriage. It is uncertain whether your issue shall live to succeed you.'

ELIZABETH Q. The succession is my business. The English people will not plead with me and my Parliament when they know nothing of it.

CECIL *comes through the crowd, approaches* ELIZABETH Q.

CECIL. Parliament will restrict funds until you name a successor.

ELIZABETH Q. Crown money belongs to the Crown; it will not be used as leverage by Parliament against the Monarchy.

CECIL. Parliament, Privy Council and the Monarchy are a trinity – that must operate carefully and in balance – to the benefit of the English people.

ELIZABETH Q. An absolute monarch ought not to be accountable for their actions to anyone other than God.

Beat.

CECIL. There are MPs who support those who move against you. We must, as the government of this country, consider what security we offer those generations who will come after us. The people of England need a plan for the future about which they can feel sure.

ELIZABETH Q. You can reassure them /

CECIL. / There is little that will reassure them except for a named successor.

ELIZABETH Q. And if there isn't one?

Beat.

CECIL. Privy Council and Parliament would be moved to declare a bill that offered emergency powers to the Privy Council and Parliament, in the event of the death of the monarch.

ELIZABETH Q. God decides who rules this country. It is a king or a queen – chosen by God and invested with God's divinity.

Beat – stand-off.

No councillor, minister or /

CECIL (*shouting*). / Government has to govern if you will offer us no answer. If you will not marry and have children, then something, must be done – to construct some feeling of security!

ELIZABETH Q. And this construction of security, just so happens to leave you in charge?

Pause.

CECIL. Not if you'd agreed to marry King Philip.

ELIZABETH Q. / The thing about marriage, Cecil – the thing about it, is that Mary Queen of Scots – my cousin – her husband, who she married, for safety – like you're telling me to, turned out to be a drunkard and a murderer. Then he, Darnley, was murdered, for being a murderer – and Mary, in her wisdom, so terrified of being alone – decided her murderous first husband's murderer – was safe harbour – and so she married him. He, to no one's huge surprise, raped her and beat her and imprisoned her, a queen, so badly – that she was thrown on the mercy of her people. Her people told her she could either abdicate or they would drown her in a sack. It was at that point that she came begging to me, her cousin, who had to imprison her. I just feel like we should interrogate, for a tiny second, the presumed definition of marriage as safety. It hasn't kept Mary very safe, has it?

CECIL. It's safer than standing alone.

ELIZABETH Q. How can I be queen of a country and subject to a husband.

CECIL. Your marriage would be an alliance that creates strength and unity between countries.

ELIZABETH Q. I don't need an alliance – I am Head of the Church and Queen of England.

CECIL. Governor, Your Majesty – you are not Head – you are Governor. Which King Philip would tolerate.

Eighteen

Late.

ELIZABETH Q *sits – thinks, stares. Feels very alone.*

DUDLEY *enters.*

DUDLEY. Bess?

ELIZABETH Q. You're banished. You should be in Kew.

DUDLEY. There's something you should know.

ELIZABETH Q. You can't help.

DUDLEY. The girl. Please. She's upset. She's crying. She came to me.

ELIZABETH Q. What?

DUDLEY. I said I'd try and help her.

　　DUDLEY *exits.*

ELIZABETH Q (*calling after him*). What are you doing? Dudley?

　　DUDLEY *re-enters with* KATHERINE. KATHERINE *is six months pregnant.*

　　ELIZABETH Q *stares.* KATHERINE *tries to leave.*

　　What is this?

KATHERINE. A baby.

DUDLEY. Please. Go gently.

ELIZABETH Q. It's treason.

KATHERINE. I love him.

DUDLEY (*realises*). It's not me, no – no – no. Fuck no. (*Trips over one of the steps.*) It's Hertford's kid. The Earl of Hertford.

　　Long pause – ELIZABETH Q *stares at her, tries to compute what this means.*

ELIZABETH Q. You are the Queen's cousin and you are with child by a nobleman without the Queen's permission.

KATHERINE (*drops to her knees*). No. No. It's not treason,
I swear to you – I swear. We met, and it was really quick,
I just – we talked, like you said, but I felt so many things –
and I just couldn't stop thinking about him, all the time, like
I was on fire with it and then, when saw each other, I was
trying to be – but I couldn't.

ELIZABETH Q. The child is a bastard? It is illegitimate?

KATHERINE. We took a boat across the river, one lunchtime,
over to Cannon Row and we got this priest, off the street –
and we were married.

DUDLEY *steps into protect* KATHERINE.

ELIZABETH Q. Why have you brought her here? Just take her
straight to the Tower.

KATHERINE *falls to the floor, screaming*.

KATHERINE. No! Please!

ELIZABETH Q. Shut up. I've got a headache.

DUDLEY. Who suggested you should have Blanche Parry read
your palm and when she did, she encouraged that you get
married?

KATHERINE. Cecil.

DUDLEY. And who has been telling you to report to him about
the welfare of your baby – for some months?

KATHERINE. Cecil.

DUDLEY. And who came to speak to your father about it in
June?

KATHERINE *looks nervously at* DUDLEY.

Tell her.

KATHERINE. Cecil.

DUDLEY. It is an attempt at overthrow. The family call him
uncle.

KATHERINE. It's not I swear, I swear it! My intentions were only ever romantic, nothing ambitious or political – it was love and only love – and as such, personal and unstoppable. I am no threat to you, Your Majesty.

ELIZABETH Q. Dudley, get Cecil for me, please.

DUDLEY *exits*. ELIZABETH Q *pulls out a chair*.

You should take the weight off in your condition.

KATHERINE *sits nervously*. ELIZABETH Q *goes to fetch a plate of pineapple and a fork*.

Do you know what this is?

KATHERINE (*shakes her head*). No.

ELIZABETH Q. It's a pine-*a*pple. It's new.

KATHERINE *nods slowly*.

Do you know how hard Drake had to work to get it? Can you imagine what it must be like to risk your life getting to a place that you don't really know exists? All those days, at sea, just reaching for it.

ELIZABETH Q *pops the pineapple in* KATHERINE*'s mouth – she takes it, nervously*.

They say this strange fruit can precipitate labour.

KATHERINE *clamps her mouth shut against the pineapple*.

What was it about the Earl of Hertford that made you betray me?

KATHERINE. He came to meet me and we went for a walk and he took my hand and he rested it in his lap and we sat and looked up through the trees into the big blue sky and we just sat, like that, for ages – and we listened to the wind.

DUDLEY *and* CECIL *enter partway through and are captivated by it*.

ELIZABETH Q. Go on.

KATHERINE. He kissed me. He said he hoped it worked out and asked that I might meet his mother. I agreed and something – sort of silently – felt like hope. Just a fraction of it – felt like the harvest due to be in, or the way the sun catches dust in the air just before autumn, I looked at him and I don't know why – but I just really trusted him, I thought we could make a family. He felt like home.

ELIZABETH Q. And where is he, now? This man?

KATHERINE. He fled to France as soon as he heard I was with child.

ELIZABETH Q. Send her to the Tower.

KATHERINE. No.

ELIZABETH Q. Take the child away as soon as it is born. If the husband returns, jail them separately. She's a fucking idiot.

KATHERINE. I'd rather die than not see my husband.

ELIZABETH Q. Don't be so stupid!

KATHERINE. You love men more than anyone does; you can tell from how you either fear them or let them rule you.

ELIZABETH Q *rams the fork, hard, through the back of* KATHERINE'*s hand. She screams. It goes right through.*

DUDLEY. Jesus!

ELIZABETH Q. Take her away!

CECIL *takes* KATHERINE.

CECIL. He needs to be gone before I get back.

ELIZABETH Q. You are in no position to be accusing people of being a threat to the throne.

CECIL. Get up! Go!

CECIL *and* KATHERINE *leave.*

ELIZABETH Q *sits, stares.*

DUDLEY. If you don't have a child, they'll keep coming.

ELIZABETH Q. Is that an offer?

DUDLEY. It can be. If you want it to be.

ELIZABETH Q. Some envious noble would kill you.

DUDLEY. I don't know if I much care. King doesn't really interest me. I just want to be with you.

ELIZABETH Q. You don't feel fear. You can sleep anywhere. I haven't slept properly since I was three. They left me with a nurse who fell asleep, during my mother's execution. It got so dark – and I was too small to light the candles, I couldn't reach. Ever since. The dark has terrified me. Terrified. You live for it.

DUDLEY. I love you.

ELIZABETH Q. I know you do. It's mutual. It doesn't mean that I can trust you or that the country would be safe.

You are my weakness. My greatest want. My weakest thing.

Every part of me that doesn't want you – is stronger for it. The piece of me that wants you – is ferocious, in its weakness, and in danger of taking over the rest of me – all the time. If I want to be made of something, I have to resist you. As much as I want to evaporate, most days – to wash myself away in the stream of you – I have to continue existing. Because I am a queen. I was put on earth for other things. Stronger things. Calmer things. And these are the things that I have to do. (*Beat.*) And so – you have to leave.

Beat.

DUDLEY *leaves.*

ELIZABETH Q *tries to breathe, exhales very slowly.*

CECIL *returns.*

Did you back Katherine Grey to take the throne?

CECIL. No.

ELIZABETH Q. And what do I do if I don't believe you?

CECIL. Execute me. (*Pause.*) Mary Queen of Scots has had a baby boy.

ELIZABETH Q. How lovely.

CECIL. The power of Catholic Europe has got behind it, there is a planned invasion from Spain, backed by the Papacy, to put Mary on your throne. Mary has condoned it. You must have her executed.

ELIZABETH Q. Absolute monarchs ought not to be accountable for their actions to anyone other than God.

CECIL. We have written proof of Mary's will to assassinate you.

ELIZABETH Q. I will not kill a queen.

Nineteen

ELIZABETH Q. Best not to panic. If you can avoid it. They tell
   you you have to marry before your face runs out, you have to
   have babies before your body runs out –

My mother was so desperate to have a male heir, that she slept
   with her brother. That's panic – isn't it? It worked, she got
   pregnant, but she caught my father sleeping with somebody
   new and the fear of it – overtook her – and she lost the baby.
   At sixteen weeks. It was a boy. My father told her she'd
   miscarried her saviour. They went ahead and executed her
   a couple of weeks later. They tell you to cling to things...

WASHERWOMAN *enters*.

Hello.

WASHERWOMAN. Sorry, Your Majesty, I thought the room
   was empty.

ELIZABETH Q. –

WASHERWOMAN. I'm collecting your sheets, I'm from the
   laundry.

ELIZABETH Q. You sell them information, don't you? About
   whether I still bleed, monthly – I hear the Spanish are
   particularly interested?

Beat.

I mean, I know you do – so /

WASHERWOMAN. / It's just they offered me so much more
   than I could make any other way.

ELIZABETH Q. I've stopped. Bleeding. You can tell them.
   They can stop asking.

WASHERWOMAN. I see.

ELIZABETH Q. I am born of woman but no child shall come
   from me.

WASHERWOMAN. Right. (*Beat*.) You okay?

ELIZABETH Q. Grief – obviously – a bit, the idea of – family or something, but – at least they'll stop pestering me. Have you got children?

WASHERWOMAN. Three. But none survived past. They all died early.

ELIZABETH Q. I'm sorry.

WASHERWOMAN. It's how it goes. Isn't it.

Often. No point moaning about it or the Queen wouldn't get her clean sheets.

ELIZABETH Q. Right.

ELIZABETH Q *nods solemnly,* WASHERWOMAN *goes to leave.*

When bad things actually happen.

WASHERWOMAN. Yes?

ELIZABETH Q. It's one less thing to fear.

ELIZABETH Q *takes the ring and hands it to the* WASHERWOMAN.

WASHERWOMAN. What's this?

ELIZABETH Q. I don't want you to be out of pocket now there's no information to sell.

WASHERWOMAN. I don't want to be – uh – but you're the Queen of England and you still feel… so I'm not sure money is the answer. You can keep it.

ELIZABETH Q *puts the ring back on her finger.*

WASHERWOMAN *turns to leave.*

ELIZABETH Q. What can I give you?

WASHERWOMAN. Nothing, thank you.

WASHERWOMAN *is almost gone – when she stops.*

When you pick up that crown and it's got all those rubies on it – that would feed people for weeks – do you really believe, like in your bones, that God wants you to wear that on your head more than he wants you to feed all those people? Like you do know, at some level, it's just a hat – and you're just a person – No?

ELIZABETH Q. When you take communion, on a Sunday – the wine you drink, is it wine – or blood?

Pause.

WASHERWOMAN. Tastes like wine.

ELIZABETH Q. And do you believe that a priest can change that wine into blood?

WASHERWOMAN. Magic, if he could.

ELIZABETH Q. Can he?

WASHERWOMAN. Witchery?

ELIZABETH Q. Divinity.

WASHERWOMAN. It's all just hats. Only – priests and witches get treated very differently.

ELIZABETH Q. I was put here by God to be Queen.

WASHERWOMAN. So I must have been put here to do the sheets.

Pause.

ELIZABETH Q. And if I was just a normal woman and have – done it all anyway.

WASHERWOMAN. You've got a lot of staff and – stuff – around you.

ELIZABETH Q. But still. It's hard. It can be.

WASHERWOMAN. That'd make you something really serious.

WASHERWOMAN *leaves.*

STAGE MANAGEMENT *appear* – ELIZABETH Q *and* STAGE MANAGEMENT, *together – disrobe* ELIZABETH Q *and leave her in trousers and a jacket.*

Twenty

ELIZABETH Q. It suits you, doesn't it? That I'm put here by God. It allows you to accept that I'm not a king. My divinity, it /

CECIL. / Your Majesty.

ELIZABETH Q. Our grandfathers fought on the same battlefield. Yours went into service, mine became a king. There probably wasn't much in it.

CECIL. I am in the presence of divinity.

Beat.

ELIZABETH Q. Are you? Did you ever meet my father?

CECIL. Yes.

ELIZABETH Q. Do you feel the same way about me as you did about him?

CECIL. The fact that you have remained unmarried and we have worked, for all these years so closely, has afforded me a proximity to the Queen and a complexity of working relationship that I don't think I would have got – with a king.

ELIZABETH Q. That's intimacy. It's different.

CECIL. Preferable. Possibly. It has altered me. I have – learnt things.

ELIZABETH Q. You told me you looked after me the day my mother was executed. You didn't – I was left alone. With a nursemaid, all day. I remember it. You lied.

CECIL. I often feel the reason that you think that people love you is because you're Queen. I wanted you to know that there is something intrinsically valuable, loveable or – just precious about you – as a human.

ELIZABETH Q. I can't help but feel you were trying to manipulate me. Emotionally.

CECIL. Everything I have ever done has been to try and make you safe.

ELIZABETH Q *exits*.

Twenty-One

CECIL *offers* DUDLEY *the death warrant.*

CECIL. She's overestimating her strength.

DUDLEY. She said she didn't want to kill a queen.

CECIL. She signed the warrant.

DUDLEY. She hasn't agreed to send it.

CECIL. She's not logically assessing the scale of the threat against her.

DUDLEY. She feels loyalty to /

CECIL. / Don't get dragged into her pit of indecision. It's weak.

DUDLEY. She can't always see what's good for her.

CECIL. Or for the country.

> CECIL *hands the warrant over.*

We need to act with reason and speed.

DUDLEY. Because she is acting with neither.

CECIL. Exactly.

> DUDLEY *takes the warrant.*

Epilogue

ELIZABETH Q. They dispatched the warrant for the death of Mary Queen of Scots without asking me. Nineteen men sat in a room, in the half-dark, and went behind my back. Cecil used the Queen's seal.

ELIZABETH P. Take this – all of you – and eat it.

For this is my body which will be given up for you.

Hands the chalice to ELIZABETH Q.

Take this all of you and drink from it.

ELIZABETH Q. For this is the chalice of my blood.

Divinity.

Witchery.

Theatricality.

ELIZABETH P. This church. This temple.

ELIZABETH Q. This theatre.

ELIZABETH Q *pours blood onto the stage – in a line – Dionysian – we see it.*

Together – we get to remake things. Re-believe. Our histories.

ELIZABETH P. Childless. Unmarried.

ELIZABETH Q. Childless.

Every child in England has remembered her, for centuries.

ELIZABETH P. Unmarried?

ELIZABETH Q. The only unmarried woman to ever rule this country did it successfully – for forty-four years – she was her own safety.